DARK AGES

DARK AGES

DAVID HARTNETT

Secker & Warburg
POETRY

First published in Great Britain 1992
by Martin Secker & Warburg Limited
Michelin House, 81 Fulham Road, London SW3 6RB

Copyright © 1992 David Hartnett

The author has asserted his moral rights

A CIP catalogue record for this book
is available from the British Library

ISBN 0 436 20116 X

Set in 10/12½ Bembo
Printed in Great Britain by
St. Edmundsbury Press, Bury St. Edmunds

CONTENTS

ACKNOWLEDGEMENTS

Some of these poems have previously appeared in *Numbers*, *Sunday Times* and the *Times Literary Supplement*.

'The Lifts' won the 1989 *TLS*/Cheltenham Festival Poetry Competition and was subsequently broadcast on BBC Radio 4.

The epigraph to 'Their Starry Mirrors' is taken from George Seferis' *A Poet's Journal*.

The epigraph to 'Dark Ages' mixes brief passages from *The Anglo-Saxon Chronicle*, Masefield's 'The Rider at the Gate', Avraham Tory's *Surviving the Holocaust, The Kovno Ghetto Diary*, Harold Owen's *Journey from Obscurity* and Louis Simpson's 'I Dreamed that in a City Dark as Paris'.

SWITCHING ON LIGHTS

It is time to go up again through the dark house
Switching on lights. When, from my blind finger,
Each room streams into shape, that shape is stranger,
Briefly, for the current of nothingness
That flowed invisible there, hours before sleep.

As I grope forward I can hear the feet
Of my children on the stairs, chased by their mother;
Ripples of tired laughter drift together
All these glittering shells I secrete
On the tideline that stitches the sandy hem of sleep.

And yet should I turn they might as soon be lost,
So close their echoes wash, so remote.
Always the house conceals, its door blown shut,
A room whose darkness I know I shall have missed
Once perhaps, long into sleep or after sleep.

THE FLEECE

We went to the hovel of the midnight shearer
And lay together, naked, on a wooden board.
Swiftly his sharp-toothed comb skimmed and whirred
Peeling back the fleece our love had grown
Until it dropped away, limp in the straw,
Still warm from us, a loosened milky gown,
Though brambles snagged and blood-spots dabbed
    the wool.
I saw him knead its softness to a roll.
Then through wicket gates to a dark field
Weightless, we ran and lay together, numb.
Prickling stars of sweat our skins bristled
Until, wherever limb brushed against limb,
A luminous froth uncurled, shivered into flame.
By dawn what fleece had clothed us, new or old?

INTO THE SEA-ROOM

Lead me, your fingers laced against my eyes,
Down into the sea-room. Let me guess
How autumn storms have pyramided shoals
Of flint-grey photos, letters scoured as shells.

Then let me hear the hiss white minutes make
Receding, peeling their braided chevrons back
Round wrack of crumpled stockings, pearls, a
    slip . . .
I will lick at the salt tufting each fingertip

Until their pink quills suddenly all splay
Showing me the sea-room sunk into the sea,
Floors of a far glass wilderness where you wade
Naked, toward me now, thighs thonged with weed.

GARLIC

Come to the shed door where autumn light
Yellows against the darkness, kneading it –
I am squatted beyond the light, plaiting garlic.

The bulbs are so papery thin they yield no hint
Of the moist heat their mauve half-moons ovened
Underground three seasons. Come to the door

And, leaning, let your creamy-petalled skirt
Mould its crumpled cone against a sickle
Of thigh, a buttock's pivoting of corm.

Today I can barely remember the first time
A raw clove seared my tongue or the first time
Our tongue-tips merged to share their meal of juices.

Night after night we would peel and crush the corms
Swathing sticky tissues with warm oils
Then lean to taste each other's strangenesses.

Now however we lie half melted together
Our bodies have sealed each other so tightly in
One touch releases all the old salt-sweetness.

A winter is coming when the last shrivelled globe
Must hang dangling silvery roots, white hair . . .
Whoever comes to pluck it shivers at the door

Then turns back into the dark. Must it be me
Love, or you, or just the shadows we cast
Against this yellowing light, autumns before?

Raised to adjust a hairgrip your underarm
Slides on tufted darkness. The bulbs are plaited
And still my fingers reek leaked juices. Touch them.
Smear your skin again with the odour of garlic.

THE AMMONITE

Remember the quarry,
The ammonite?
We might marry
That summer, we thought:

A coiled giant
(*Lewesiceras*)
Bedded in flint,
It took eras

Of afternoons off
To prise that white
Ribbing from the cliff.
Remember the weight

Hugged to the car
(Sunset combing
Your henna'd hair
To a copper foaming),

The suture cracks
Like curls of fern?
'76,
The drought was on:

Serpent bolts
Rifting walls,
Shadowy faults
In parched soils.

Upstairs that night
Drinking your breath,
The ammonite
In the room beneath,

I saw its shell
Burn whiter
As your clothes fell,
Rustling water.

★

The lawns scorch.
Your white dress
Floats through the porch
Of the registry office.

How old we look now
In the wedding snaps,
Heavy somehow,
Rooted to the steps –

As if time's strata
Formed in the air,
Limpid as water,
Layer by layer.

Time to be done
With summer and drought,
To move, have children.
And the ammonite?

Long since lost
In a loft crate.
Yet still its ghost
May pass, a mote,

Your eye's pink lid
When we lie down
On the rippled bed.
How light we have grown,

As if – warm sea
Locked in a cliff –
Memory
Released love.

Remember the quarry,
The ammonite?
We might marry
One day, we thought.

BEETROOT

Their juice black on the back of my hand's pewter
I have been tamping all these wrinkled phials
In a box of sand: beet, this autumn's roots.

My memory knots. At midnight once her body
Emerging, wrinkled, black with blood, was pewter.
How soon I leant to that lightly swaddled weight.

Swaddled for frosts the moon's navel sheds
She lies tonight on the dark side of the house.
This box will be too full to lift soon. Soon

Ravelled by the cord of light back to a window's
Molten knot I may glimpse you leaning
Over the firebox feeding it sanitary towels,

Your face a tired pewter in the flame-roots' wrinkle.
By midnight, that stained crescent crisped to black,
Frost will have cleaved these sand-grains, sutured
    them.

NOVEMBER

The day so short, so chill,
That disc of ice
You detached in one piece
From the water-bucket's rim
This morning before school
Has lain on the grey grass
Frozen into afternoon
While, a dilating coal,
The sun simmers west.
You are coming home soon
And there will be no call
Then, still less the time,
To say how much I missed
Your voice just now, your presence,
As, touching that hard
Brittle transparence,
I felt it already furred
With the soft needle points
Of tonight's frost.

NIGHT VOYAGES

These nights you sway wide-eyed
At the cot's prow, the pharos
Of a vapouriser flares
Your face and I sense a tide
Under my heart's susurrus
Tug at your unlived years.

This world was never round.
Up the wall's pale hull
Dates and heights I have charted
Flicker as if to sound
Fathoms of bone and cell –
Your voyage has already started.

Close to this harbour boom
Owl-sirens, ghosts of sailors,
Reef the dark leagued trees;
When I lean into your bedroom
The door-jambs are two pillars,
Rootless, pouring seas.

THE GREEK HELMET

Giving you the Bible today I forgot
Its flyleaf drawing done in blue ink:
A horsehair-crested, visored Greek helmet,
      The kind I think

They wore at the battle of Thermopylae.
I was your age. At first my school, being new,
Seemed ancient in its strangeness (as yours may)
      And so I drew

This charm or threat. Look out through its sockets:
Where bonfire smoke twists to turbid gloom
Behind the goal, a boy waits, hands in pockets –
      He longs for home.

Look again. Heat shudders the cricket pitch
Outside the classroom where he sits alone,
Wanting nothing more than time to watch
      Dust climb the sun.

Say that this ancient history has faded,
Yet still, like the air smoke or motes pass through,
Those days, once remembered, seem threaded
      With love for you.

Take them, taking this, so when you come
To overscore, as you must, the Greek helmet
With fresh drawing, their light will thread the charm,
      Their dark the threat.

COUNTING NAPPIES

Dry now at three and a half you wake near dawn
And take yourself to the bathroom. Sleepy,
I lie and consider the long reign of the nappy:
How many must we have changed since your brother
    was born?

That was seven years ago and every day
At first there would be six, so multiply
Three-six-five by seven to get . . . not yet,
Now maths whitens to a room, a changing mat

Where, changelessly emollient, the ritual
Of waste and wipe and sticky tab bows me above
Limbs so strange so familiar I cannot tell
Anymore my love from weariness, my love.

You have flushed the bowl and run to bed again,
The cistern's tide ebbs for a new reign.
I dream of white, bleached duvets folded to dough,
To limbs that thicken, change . . . then suddenly know

That we will have no more children; that the room
Where you and your brother lay has disappeared,
Your change still changing us; that what I feared
This dawn was less to count nappies than uncount time.

JACKDAWS

Spring again and again, their clamped beaks gilled
With twigs, two jackdaws work blue straits dividing
The wood from our house; by now they have half filled
The mouth of the study flue with their loose braiding
While down onto the hearth the stray sticks patter
Heaping a pyre, chill dormancies of matter.

A room off, deep into afternoon our daughter
Sleeps, hot coals aflutter in either cheek.
Birth washed her here, withdrew, yet she hears water
Still, by the hearth, head tilted, plucking a stick
And poising it in her palm as if to douse
For streams that, lapping, flow beyond this house.

She hears the jackdaws too: their muffled squeal
Of almost human anger when the nest
Sheds back into our world makes her smile
As, hooded by the throat of the chimney breast,
She sways on the bed of an ocean shoaled with wings
Or crackles through this wrack's enkindlings.

Four hundred years ago a Tudor child
Tilted its head, too, listening. Then as now
The house creaked like a ship moored in the Weald,
While over the green waves jackdaws flew
Hatched to outlive all owners brood by brood,
Branch-freighted djinn, familiars of the flood.

And yet a leather shoe that child wore once
Came down to us, new owners, newer parents;
Bricked up, a fertility charm, for generations
Close to the nesting flue until time's currents
Washed it out one day, a calcined coal,
The wraith of a foot's whorl ferning its fossil sole.

Still strange the house made us strangers a little
That dawn I woke to your breath's quick ember
Pulsing against my cheek, then heard the brittle
Crackling of flames downstairs. Remember?
The house invisible, a jackdaw went
Fluttering from wall to window, eyes aglint.

I set him loose; and still his squabs' squabs stoke
The pyre, kindling enough for an hour or two
Although that nest would make the fire smoke . . .
Home from school our son kicks off a shoe
That drums against the chimney and lies still.
Pluck it and you shiver in the updraught's chill.

Jackdaws, watching, not watching who comes, is
    gone,
That earth your iridescences in a wall
Yet layer stones with air, some distant dawn
When I wade from these rooms let a twig fall
So I may glance up briefly, knowing the path,
Random, deliberate, may finish in a hearth.

CLUSTER FLIES

Winter: dusk by four,
Yet still they emerge to fret
The windowpane, drape
A shawl of beaded jet
Over the sill across the floor;
Will they ever stop?

And always this death by twitches
Occurs in one room
Unused at the back of the house:
A smoke-bay once, floorless,
Hooks on a charred beam
For hanging flitches.

They must breed up in the loft,
Among the horsehair and dung
Panels: curers' chambers
Perhaps, but no one remembers.
How might those people have lived?
I try imagining

Only to unlock
A room within a room –
Something hangs from a hook,
Something crawls across the floor,
Something begins to swarm,
Dirtying the air.

Tonight after I had hoovered
Up the latest scree,
Rain from a flint of wind
Sparked and I shivered:
Around the bulb one fly,
Hatched out already, droned.

THE APPLE STORE

Morning is vestal in the whitewashed shrine.
I enter from blue frost to check the flame
Each green maid tends, mouthing her sacred name:
Laxton's, Crawley Beauty, Cornish Pine.
But suddenly the light goes tense and sere –
Before me sprawls a rusting ulcerous trove
Flung by shadows out of the black grove
Into the black lake of the dying year.
I fear them then, laid in that leprous tomb,
I fear their alchemies of must and froth,
Cankerous distillations that consume
Themselves in a sour perpetual earthiness:
O Ashmead's Kernel, Cox, Beauty of Bath;
Orleans Reinette, Kidd's Orange Red, Charles Ross.

★

But to return still fearful in the night:
Far ocean night down which the oak-leaf shoals –
Fang-finned, sere-gilled go threading capsized hulls
Of barns that blunt the blade of rain-scratched light
My hot torch smelts. They are so heavy now,
So drowned in silt of November's deep-sea trench,
They green to geodes pulsing on the bench,
Night's waters stained with their benthonic glow.
O Ashmead's Kernel, I am stained as well,
Heavy my Crawley Beauty, hard to move . . .
The wind devours my torch's jaundiced jewel
And suddenly shell by carunculated shell,
The apples rise up floating from their grave:
Russet-fleshed mermaids, doomed to drown or save.

TRAVELLER'S TALE

When you arrive
In that winter kingdom's
Rutted march,

Visit the grey
Unguarded chalk-
And-asbestos palace:

Though rapt in dining,
Petalled round a hopper,
Once alerted,

The bristly princesses
Will turn, press forward,
Munching hay-gold.

For that is their custom
When strangers approach
The rust-tettered rail —

Which you must honour
Stroking slippery
Salmon-pink muzzles

Splayed for the reech
And fume of greeting;
Fondling fuzzy

Tumuli set
On lazily tilted
Dehorned foreheads.

But to gaze deep
In a full unblinking
Blond-lashed moon;

Or linger too long
By concrete clamps
Where the tarnished green

Treasuries
Of copper dung
Trickle black,

Is to risk never
Going home again,
Or home so changed

Each day will seem
A yard of exile,
Each night a stall

Where, waking on straw,
Naked and bound,
You sense beyond

The water trough's
Sarcophagus drip,
Gentle, unhurried,

Vigilant shadows
That cough and shuffle,
Shuffle and cough.

ROLLO

Dry for weeks
The day you died,
But in the run
The peacock displayed
His feathers rustling
And I heard rain.

Each pinion
Was the greenish gold
Ray of a rising
Never risen sun.
Your legs were stiff,
Your fur cold.

You lay as if dozing
On the patio;
Nearby, the fountain,
Its scummy cushion
I had seen you nosing
A day ago;

At nostril and mouth
A thin brown froth
The flies savoured.
Kidneys I said
But my son cried
For this first death.

And, as he spilled
A trickle of milk
On your tamped clay,
I saw you play
With the fox-cubs again
In a dusk field.

That afternoon
The vixen returned.
She left one hen,
Her oviduct ripped:
Two eggs inside,
A yolky blood.

That night thunder
But still no rain,
The peacock miaowing,
The earth a cracked gong.
I listened, knowing
Your resonance gone.

FAWNS

I should have known it was no rabbit scream.
That the body my dog had been flinging up and
    mouthing
Was neither small nor grey enough. By the time
I had run back the fawn lay slack-tongued, still.
But I found another near the hedge wide-eyed,
    breathing,
The delicate folded legs tipped with coal.
I scooped him up like a cat and, feeling no wound,
Knew he would live now if his mother returned.
And indeed, half an hour later, watching from the
    ride,
I saw him totter to her. She saw I saw
But what she made of my smell licking his hide
Or understood of her loss in the trampled grass
I could not know who passed with nothing more
Than alien words, a moment's mournfulness.

INLIERS

(The Valais Canton, New Year's Eve)

Tonight when you sow the peaks with a chrome fire
Or send the maenad rockets up to shred
Their arcing net of shrieks through clammy air,
Ignore us as you would your own dead.

Under the stonecrop screes where dying spruces
Drop scaled turds of cones, our company
– Though fewer each year and feebler – still passes
From hand to claw to fin the sleepless eye.

Caught in its lens that very light whose growth
You celebrate tonight, is black and old;
You have crossed already into your last myth
And we shall not survive to hear it told.

Tribes of the four-wheel drive, the drum machine;
Digital trolls, petroleum nibelungs,
Bilge down glaciers glittering sick of tin
Or flay with acid petals the piedmont's lungs –

Still, each of you like a child shall wake one morning
To stare at what he had yearned for night after night:
A purity so poisoned by his yearning
It cannot be owned nor fled nor wept out of sight.

THE WASPS' NEST
IN THE SHED

Ducking through the open door out of the rain
I came face to face with an empty wasps' nest
Pasted to the roof. One spring, five years ago,
Hammering the shed together in the clearing
I could imagine days spent writing there,
But when had I returned since, ever sat down?

The wasps had come: deft mouths and mandibles
Turbanning wet pulp to a paper planet.
All one summer where the grey belly tapered
Down to its orifice they must have ribboned
In and out, those plunderers of rot
And the overripe, until a first frost bit.

The rain was easing now. Whatever kept me
So long away I knew would hardly bear
My lingering now, yet to touch that husk once more
Was to sway with a brief weightlessness as if
A few of the different words I might have found
    once
Hovered there still, unshaped, inaudible.

THEIR STARRY MIRRORS

i.m. George Seferis

At Karatay, a mosque and Indje minaret, the dome open to the sky and, underneath, a square cistern, dried up now, where once they studied in the water the mirrored movement of the stars; one thinks of nights with faces leaning over, transfixed there.

One thinks of nights with faces leaning over
Studying star-tracks in the cistern's mirror.
The cistern has gone dry and he is dead.

One thinks of nights his face must have leant over
Paper's sea-white mirror, tracking black words
Back down wakes of exile into the fire.

The cistern has gone dry and he is dead.
Beyond the known world's shores, Odysseus
Voyages with a broken astrolabe and a pencil.

One thinks of nights . . . of Smyrna, Cyprus,
   Troy . . .
Of black shores and white faces, mirrored in fire:
No stars will ever light their voyage back.

The cistern has gone dry. His poems lie
Washed by a shoreless white, light's undersea.
Their starry mirrors quench our leaning faces.

AT RARON

Rose, oh reiner Widerspruch . . .

All the princesses are gone
And the chill torrents that poured
Out down the Illgraben's rubble cone;
Perched below glaciers, above the Rhone,
You who for a lifetime feared
The mirror's grip have disappeared
Now into a headstone's stone reflection.

This rock that citadels your homelessness . . .
All round a white-cross forest petrifies,
Its leaves of polythened photographs dripping tears
Of condensation from eyes
Blind to a grief gone posthumous.
So many later deaths these later years,
Your life recedes, unmournable, a source.

Easier to rehearse
That winter dawn they buried you, the ice-
Teeth gripping a water trough's blue skin
On the steep path out of the village; your coffin
Afloat behind a man with a wooden cross.
The world shrinking, the church tower swaying –
Above, white peaks, unfurled: a snowy wing.

Easier to recite
These mirror words, your epitaph.
Dragged by the wind, thorns of the same rose
That pricked your blood to illness
Down in the garden at Muzot, pluck to erase
Words that might have been carved inside a cave
To carillon silence, the echo of light.

At last I left your difficult death,
Descending to the eye of the buried lake
Whose waters feed each glistening arc that sprays
The vineyard with a meteor track.
There in the vaulted porch I saw the moon-
    mouthed trout seethe
And deeper, by the Virgin's shrine, awoke
Syllables that seemed never to stop dripping
    through a dark space.

THE LIFTS

Pity the lifts
When they slide alone
In their windy shafts
From dusk until dawn.

Each glowing deck
Is freighted with air
Yet their cables creak;
They have to take care –

These Marie Celestes
Of the midnight hotel –
That their cargo of ghosts
Does not roll:

The face someone shed
Between two floors;
Words beheaded
By corridors;

The brief Hiroshima
Of body heat
Flaying a mirror;
A lipsticked heart;

Dust-cauls; perfume;
The birthmark that laughed;
Faeces of sperm;
Pity the lift

A sleepwalker passes,
Its pad of pink nipples
He barely caresses,
Its rib-cage that ripples

To diamond doors
Tickled by fingertips
Brailling for stairs.
The doors will collapse

On the mercury tear
Aquiver in its stone
Thermometer;
The sleepwalker turn

Up stairs that descend
To the cellar on the roof
Smiling, blind . . .
For this is the life

And death of lifts
From dusk until dawn
In their windy shafts
Sliding alone.

INHALER

Too hard a nipple, too void an orifice
Either to suck or lick, you merely want
My finger and parted lips so that your cloud
Of bitter calming gas can again be spilled
Down passageways to where I lie, a child.
Shapechanger, plastic and metal, rubber once, glass,
One-eyed harbinger, we have gone back to bed
Together so many times I have lost count:
Tell me, then, after our voyage of thirty years,
What moons of preterknowledge or regret
Drag at these lungs, making their lavers hiss
And tighten as breath's tide, sighing, withdraws?
What is this siren whose song can suffocate?
Or tell me nothing except that I must press.

DEAD ON FOUR

I heard my sleeping child laugh in the dark
And woke with the dream of the underground carpark
Where someone chases me from floor to floor.
I could not sleep. My watch glowed dead on four.

I wish I hadn't told him about Pompeii,
About the buried houses and the streets
And the choked people writhing perpetually
In their stiff ash dresses, their lava suits.

Someone is chasing me round the ash carpark.
He wants to boast of a bunker he has built.
But I can hear children crying in the dark:
Quick, we must catch their tears or they'll be spilt.

I wish I hadn't woken dead on four.
I wish I hadn't been reading about the War.
If all the dead in the earth were ghosts in the sky
A child might laugh before it learned to cry.

The dead are choking in the lava carpark,
They dream someone has built ovens as hot
As Vesuvius' crater and twice as dark.
They dream that they will wake but they will not.

Why was Lodz rechristened Litzmannstadt?
What if he has risen from the scorched stone vat?
I heard my child laughing in his sleep
And woke up dead on four not daring to sleep.

AS IF IT WERE
CHILD'S PLAY

You give me the acorn cup:
Pearled inside, a dewdrop
Spoons your face, reversed.
As if it were child's play
Imagine Oberon
Sipping at the elfin feast.

Hunched in the square with the rest
I queued for soup at dawn
Crying when the soup was gone
As if it were child's play
Imagine a spoon's smear
On tin, a licked tear.

You give me the berberis bead:
Its puckered skin still bloomed
With the whorl of your thumb pad.
As if it were child's play
Imagine Puck threading
Berries on a looped web.

First I fell out of the truck
Then a Ukrainian ripped
Mother's necklace off
As if it were child's play
Imagine welts his thumbs
Spidered round her neck.

You give me the moss cushion:
Snagged in its green wires
Your hair drags a gold scratch.
As if it were child's play
Imagine Titania
Her white body, sleeping.

Before they put my body
To sleep they stole my hair
They stole my one gold filling
As if it were child's play
Imagine a shower room
With scratch-marks on the ceiling.

You reach up and give me your hand
To take into my hand
As if it were child's play
As if it were child's play
The dead they shovelled away
Reach up and take this hand.

COLLABORATORS

But Captain S, although you propose reading
To class again from your longhand war memoirs –
We were the first in that camp, it would need a Dante –
I too need words. 'It is June. Ribs of old walls
Stir beneath the playing-field's ashen skin;
The hypocaust in the cellar scuttles away
On a thousand tiled stumps into darkness.'

But Monsieur G, whether or not you fought
In the Resistance, were caught, interrogated
Under torture – *They tied my arms and* – Please,
Don't sneer if I take Kipling down from the shelves
Once more. 'When lightning quenches the library lamps
Swastikas swarm from their spines to thunder's cell;
A winged face squeals "confess" on the oak fireplace.'

But Major T, the fact I never witnessed
That execution outside Singapore
– *They had stuffed it in his mouth like a bag of sweets* –
Doesn't mean you have to shake with malarial laughter
Still at my 'Boy's Own' tales. 'The wind gibbers
Now through the ranked wire lockers of the changing
      room;
The haunted footbath swirls with mud, then rust.'

And you who survived them, child, collaborator
In all these wars – *Since then my mind has failed
To dig a way in or out; Always this sound
Of fluttering; I change my shirt but my heart sweats* –
Go to sleep now, like a child. 'Bats are circling
The classroom huts; a spade simmers in the moon;
All night grey mowings steam from their matted clamps.'

THE DIORAMA

Away in Germany *on business*
You posted the diorama to my ward;
Still *under observation*, faintly bored,
I held it up to the light, squinted, pressed.
Inside, printed on a disc, the pictures passed:
Cities of a land where now you fought and won
Your high-tech wars, yet starved and ruinous
When you were not my father, I your son.
Where had they risen from, these unscarred homes
On craterless streets: the past or that new world
I sensed perhaps your absence strove to build?
The disc had rotated back to its first frames.
Soon my bed would become the battlefield
For D–Day soldiers raked by Stuka bombs.

*

The night nurse had long since cleared my troops
    away.
Beside the Rhine, a city at my back,
Black water mirroring stars, I heard you call
And suddenly the sky burned with flak.
Did you fly home, was I discharged next day?
Three decades on and the empire that you built
Through boardroom conquest, microchip assault,
May last the millennium, outlast us all.
Father I guard your gift yet when I peer
Inside each prospect shrinks to the same room,
Its window framing rubble, an upturned pram;
Where are the fountains now, the plane-tree square?
And why, as the disc rotates, do I seem to hear
A child weeping in a ward about a dream?

TRESPASSERS

At three a.m. I wake beside the pond
Next to the perimeter fence of the Lodz ghetto.
I am still in my pyjamas. There is a sound
Of wings and engines. I must take a photo

Of the green BMW cabriolet
Parked at the ghetto entrance since midday.
But the white gander has the grey's neck in his beak:
He is thrashing his wings down so the neck will break.

A VIP sits in the passenger seat.
His uniform is grey, his licence plate
Reads *SS 1*. His name is Heinrich Himmler.
In the orange moon serrated beaks glimmer.

Wrenching the two apart I tuck the stunned
Grey's trembling body under my arm.
Around my neck, uncovered, already wound,
My camera holds an AGFA colour film.

Hands at their backs twelve figures ring the car.
Their leather boots are bright but they look bored.
A thirteenth in their midst wears a yellow star
Sewn to his breast. The terrible white bird

Is shrieking triumphantly with neck erect.
Chaim Rumkowski, the Eldest of the Jews
Listens to the Reichsführer's soft words and bows.
The pinions of the grey gander are flecked.

With black where the beak clamped. One wing hangs
    slack.
Now I must put him down on the moonlit stones
To catch his enemy. An officer turns,
Nods. They will not mind the shutter's click.

Himmler is growing restless. The dull ring
Of officers snaps apart in the Heil salute.
Rumkowski bows. I screw one eye up, shoot.
I have caught the white gander by one wing

And now, a chalky duster, he is puffing
Over the fence. The cavalcade starts moving
Back to the Aryan zone. An orange beak,
The moon serrates water in the gander's wake.

The enemies are parted. It is still midday.
My grey pyjamas are smeared with a thin green dung.
Hunched in his dog-cart, Rumkowski rattles away.
The grey has tucked his head under one wing.

★

This was the sleeplessness, that the dream;
That the print but this the negative.
Ambivalent lens, chill onlooker, forgive
My feathered familiars their moonlit game

You cannot; nor yet the moon her orange light
Glowing in the night's dark room; nor yet the night
Each one of her twelve shallow acid baths
Where flattened faces surface to fresh deaths;

But, since these words are phantoms nothing haunts
And since your film survived, so that one glance
Last night at its reproduction in a book
Was enough to make certain I would wake

At three a.m. by the pond where grey and white
Struggled, watched by a shadow with furled wings,
Photographer, guilty or not, who else might
Forgive this poem, if not its trespassings?

SCHOOL OF NIGHT

Go to the school of night
In a flint-mine hall
Sit the black exam

A hoard of flaked axes
Rings your desk and paper
Answer three questions

What rustles in the lab
Who haunts the armoury
The cannibals where are they

Locusts their thoraxes
Honeying the glass tank
Words for a child crying

Soldiers with oiled pull-throughs
Threading silver barrels
Wars for a child crying

Under the cricket pitch
In the causewayed camp's ditch
Wraiths for a child crying

Hand in your paper
The ink was invisible
The pen a scraper

Sleep on the bell-barrow's berm
Shaken before dawn
By Somme shelling

DARK AGES

The setting is Sussex, the Somme, Germany,
Eastern Europe: the time that of two World Wars,
the withdrawal of the Roman legions, a fifties
childhood ... Grandparents appear, parents, soldiers,
tyrants, ghosts . . . There is a beach, a house, a hill . . .

(A windy night was blowing on Rome
Rumours sprang up again about pits dug in the fort
In this year Aelle came to Britain

These wars have been so great, they are forgotten
He did not rise and I saw that he was involuntarily immobile
In this year Aelle came to Britain
And the cressets guttered on Caesar's home)

This is the past: a beach, low hills inland.
She holds a thermos plugged with silver foil.
The forts of your saxon shore are built from sand.

Ask her about that ack–ack saraband
The fighters danced; the primus pan may boil
Over but this is her past, she'll understand

How, *beneath the hill's clenched mauve hand,*
Mercenaries at dusk divide their spoil
In the rubble of a saxon shore fort built on sand.

Then ask what was that song's name the band
Played on the quay when all the world was loyal.
But this is a past she does not understand:

How, *when the ice-cream van comes wailing, fanned*
Flame-throwers drive from dug-outs men of soil
Along a smoky shore's tyre-churned sand.

The waves' white tesserae crumble. Strand by strand,
She has pinned her silver hair up in a coil
And vanished inside the cold thermos. Unmanned,
All your forts are filling with grains of sand.

★

The house is lit. You feel the dead begin
Pulling you by the sleeve up the flint path.
However slow you walk no one is in,

Except the mosaic dancing girl's mist djinn,
Risen from her melted hole, the squatters' hearth.
This is my house whose atrium dead begin

A war. I hide in its hypocausts, my skin
Mottled to blue in their dry and ashen bath.
How slowly you walked here, but no one is in

Now that Aella has set sail from Berlin.
Listen to the wind's siren. It is not worth
Defending this house razed by our dead. Begin

To hoard your plastic soldiers in a tin;
Then seek the camp re-fortified at your birth
By my ancestors – some may still be in

The shadow of slumped ramparts. Fin by fin
The mosaic's bloody shoals snout their earth
Whose house goes dark now. Feel the dead begin
Pushing you away: for no one else is in.

*

Samian sherds still fleck the Virginia creeper
In autumn's empire. The sun-lounge is so warm
He has had to cover his face with a newspaper.

Through glass you watch the mosaic gorgon seep her
Bladderwrack snakes under his chair. You came
Bearing a broken tea-cup. But the creeper

Rustles a dead face: the demobbed sapper
Who drove you once from the berm of the muddy
    stream
Waving his wire shears and a scrolled paper.

Keep out. For I knew Mithras. My yellow taper
Gutters upon the firestep as each bomb
Sows its sherds. Will the sun-lounge sleeper

Never wake? *I am the carrier's skipper*
Cover your eyes so the gorgon's crown may bloom
Above their city writhing to white paper.

Emperor of autumn, evening's stormtrooper,
Rise from your ocean trench, your Ypres mausoleum
And press these sherds sloughed from the stone
    creeper
To a gorgon mask on a bible's end-paper.

★

Now you have climbed to the loft never forget
Cigar-sweet boxes packed with cotton wool
(The cracked mosaic rests on an oubliette);

Inside the hecatombs of the mist net.
Armed with his thorax pins, his cyanide phial,
Can the SS lepidopterist's ghost forget

These crumbling legions caught in flight? Not yet:
For the retiarius, buried on the hill
Under the gorgon's mosaic in an oubliette,

Will rise at dawn and come with dogs to fret
Frail shadows to the siding. *Hide in a wall
Or in a loft, I will never forget*

*To search for you. Sense how your silhouette
Behind the cold tank sheds its cobweb caul.
Your ancient mosaic is cracked, an oubliette*

Swarming with tessera tears, the gorgon's sweat.
It is dusk. A faded wing flutters its coal
Above the loft ladder. Time to forget,
The heart's cracked butterfly furled, this oubliette.

★

For hours the sun-lounge theatre echoes attack
And counter-attack he sleeps through, deckchair tilted.
In the wind the leaves of his newspaper whirr back.

Your friend has lost; deserts, his frayed rucksack
Stuffed with troops you lead. The push halted,
You chase him up the hill none can attack

Now that our mud mosaic has begun to crack
Open the miller's tomb. On its vaulted
Chamber his name is scratched. Dusk falls. Turn back

To where their wall has made a cul de sac:
One room a stove, five families, sleet unmelted;
Who can protect them from our dawn attack?

Not the tramp tamping your howitzer with a matchstick
Nor Aella and his death squad, trenchcoats felted
With cindered torah wings. Your friend is back

Tapping at the french window. But lightning's flak
Flashes across scales the gorgon moulted
For the deckchair's chestnut cairn. When winds attack
The paper he holds is white, whirring to black.

★

The bonfire sieves the dusk, its holes are sparks.
Count of the Roman candle and the wheel
He bows to its ashen rim, then folds and forks.

They are burning Aella's body not Guy Fawkes'.
His longboat has been dragged to the pagan hill.
Its pyre sieves the dusk, scattering sparks

Across the fort *where the special detail works*
Emptying every pit that had been full
To its ashen rim, bowed over wet pitchforks.

Cupped to a glow his taper's snake uncorks
The fireworks' leaping djinn, their hiss and spill
Sieving the dusk *beneath our wings with sparks,*

Tessera houses tamped in flickering darks
Of Dresden's red mosaic. What will crawl
Out of these ash-caves the gorgon forks,

Now that, the longboat burnt, his ghost embarks
From earthworks ringed with cindered tube and shell
You sieve at dawn for rocket sticks, dead sparks?
Whose is this ash the sea-wind folds and forks?

★

The miller lies in the cupboard under the stairs;
His tomb on the pagan hill is full of axes;
He is the count of all you saxon shores.

First they invaded his province, now yours:
A thumbprint in a tile; fylfot hexes
Smearing the bathhouse apse. *Under the stairs*

I grind the white flour of a thousand years:
Hair and sherds, gold spectacles in boxes —
Too many to count. Along your saxon shores,

Tamped with casts of burnt Martello towers,
Mithras will land when the mosaic moon waxes
Deathshead snakes. In the cupboard under the stairs,

The dancing girl has hidden for three years,
But now the gorgon rises, whirls her axis
Of black mirrors against all crumbling shores.

The mill and the house are one. The rain's spears
Pierce its walls. His tomb is full of foxes.
Too late to leave the cupboard under the stairs,
Or count these grains garnered from dark shores.

*

Pitch camp for winter: in the orchard grass
Black ant miletowers crumble to the red
Now he is walking on his hands round the house.

How can the tea be laid when melted glass
And lead still clot the floor from the last raid
They launched before winter and clumps of grass

Choke the gorgon's mouth? In silent cars
The SS lepidopterist's deathshead squad
Arrive at dawn to drive from every house

A fluttering swarm. The night is thunderous
With echoes of the Somme offensive. *Come inside:*
Winter nears; your legions are all grass

Rustling in flint mine craters. Ragged spores
Of frost fur the leather-thonged gauntlet dried
Runner bean bivouacs rasp. Under your house

Red ants have hoarded the eggs of a lost race.
All that they hatch will be slaves, the rest lie dead,
Camouflaged in their winter camps where grass
Is stone and stone the smoking of a house.

★

Her mauve hands flicker air, playing pontoon.
Your cards are leaves, black tumuli of winter.
The miller squats in the kitchen, carving a rune.

Twist or bust *our guns fall silent soon*
Across the channel. All evening she has leant her
Chin on the stair-rail. Downstairs at pontoon,

They will not see his ghost against the moon,
The clutched wire shears, the blue shrapnel splinter.
Aella has stormed the hill. His battle rune –

A fylfot scorched in the green mosaic of June –
Was cast when the miller took the bank. *Few saunter,*
Crossing the ghetto street's mud pontoon,

Those tessera puddles Mithras' black saloon
Crumbles at dawn. Too weak to reach the Centre,
She let her work card drop. There is no rune

To charm the years from twenty to twenty-one,
Raise ghosts or return the telegram they sent her
Now hooded legions guarding the corpse pontoon
Tamp yellow stars to Medusa's mauve-black rune.

*

All your Roman roads have vanished; follow
Autumn's agger, alignments of the wind
(Waves a slow chalk in the quarry's hollow)

Up to where, a rucksack for his pillow,
Clutching a last centurion, your friend
Sleeps in the cave. He vanishes. Follow

His last retreat to the coast by cross-dyke hollow-
Ways until on the beach-head under finned
Shoals screaming from cloud to cloud-hollow

You meet. *Our city of corn lies sacked, its yellow*
Blocks seamed with orange which, untwined,
Will be the thread the partisans must follow

Through coral hypocausts, a sewer's shallow
Chambers, where the vanquished crouch, half blind
He does not answer. A soldier, eaten hollow,

Goes rolling with the medusa on her fallow
Foreshore's mosaic glass. *Left behind*
Our legions vanish. Let wave follow
Wave into my flint's scooped sponge hollow.

★

The tramp begging at the back door landed with
    Aella.
He has belted his trench-coat with bailer twine.
Thunder sleeps in the hilltop tomb of the miller.

She takes his empty jerry can. Night's tiler,
He tessellates shadow into the stone
Step you crouch on by the back door. *Aella*

Waits in the burnt-out bathhouse of the villa
For mercenaries to detonate the mine
They dumped on the hill in no-man's land. The miller

Takes his jerry can back and her face grows paler
As snakes of lightning slide across the pane,
Hissing gorgon tears. *All day Aella*

Stood above them in the square, judge and gaoler.
Each filed past and, according to a sign,
Lived or trudged uphill to meet the miller

Who churns a bloody quern. Pillar by pillar
The chestnut peristyle he retreats down
Sheds orange flints for the back door cairn Aella
Will raise in 477 to night, the miller.

★

Out of the wind in the quarry's cave he squats
To the mauve spathe of a primus stove's boiling.
Your legions have set sail. Time to draw lots.

Soon he will climb to the fort and practise putts,
While you trace scratched fylfots in the ceiling
Of Aella's mine *whose tramp-commander squats*

In a trench seamed with flint where dawnlight clots
The first wave risen from the silence after shelling
To sort a mound of orange flakes. *The lots*

They drew in their attic hide were ammonites
Hung from his belt: snakestones, their white uncoiling
Drowned in the flood Mithras sent, *who squats*

Now on the air-raid shelter taking shots
At those in the quarry who cannot go toiling
Further with blocks of frozen seas. His lots

Are the tunnels he enters now, the quarry's roots,
As from the fort a yell answers your yelling:
Out of the wind a mauve and white thing squats
All night in that cave, hissing, drawing lots.

★

Your Roman maps are flapping in the storm
And autumn's cohorts leave by land and sea.
Retreat to bed, construct the blanket's berm.

The miller's ghost holds out still, in a form
Under the hillfort where the mercenaries lie,
Now they have taken your unmapped sleep by storm.

His HQ is your house. His uniform,
Dangling with Iron Cross and VC,
Hangs by the bed. He knows a ditch's berm

At the garden's end where cuirassed midges swarm
Across pontoons of sunlight into a sky
Contused to map the invading thunderstorm

Whose first fat drops will sprout the pillbox corm
He planted for a gatling in AD
369 on the haunted hillfort's berm.

Rally the bleeding chestnut hosts. Re-arm.
I have seen their transports scoop the estuary
To a churned mosaic. Your maps still chart their storm-
Troopers through shingle-beds to memory's berm.

★

Your watchtower is a treehouse white with frost.
The branches smoke. A dead leaf furls its ember.
The lost legion sleeps in a hypocaust.

They have fought their last battle and gone west
Along the stream. A plastic gun and limber
Lies under the treehouse, webbed with frost.

When will the demobbed sapper's blue ghost
Rise up to rally them? Will they remember
To claim the paper hoard from the hypocaust

Hidden in a thermos plugged with earth and rust
And buried by tattooed slaves one November
At dawn beneath watchtowers white with frost

On the camp's perimeter? Sound the last post.
It is centuries since their whistles made us clamber
Over the chalk berm. In the hypocaust

Aella ploughed out, the gorgon has dehisced
Mauve seed-heads for her lost legion's slumber:
Their skin is a blue mosaic, their breath the frost
That smokes down ducts of autumn's hypocaust.

★

Province of earth the rain's white legion sieves,
Your pharos slumps at dusk to a bonfire barrow
A child – his eyes smarting – stokes with leaves.

Cindered stubble gridirons the hill of graves.
One year folds in another, furrow by furrow.
I have ruled a province of rain, a march of sieves.

The foreshore's frigidarium scooped by waves
Seethes white sherds of cloud. Must I borrow
A child's dates from chronicles of leaves?

The sun-lounge and the loft are gorgon's caves
The wind invades. Who would return to harrow
This province of earth? The rain's white legion sieves

Its wars to what a child make-believes
Shivering by a bonfire, eyes gone narrow
From ash-and-ember hecatombs of leaves.

Tamp with chestnut maces the chestnut leaves'
Mosaic fire, stare at the gorgon's farrow:
Their province is the earth, their legion sieves
All chronicles to ash, choked with lives.